Understanding Your Rabbit's Habits

By Tamsin Stone

Published By T-Squared

ISBN 978-0-9543500-2-4

British Library Cataloguing in Publication Data
A catalogue record for this book is available in the British Library

Published by T- Squared,
451 Bideford Green, Linslade, Bedfordshire, LU7 2TZ

Contents

Introduction	7
Body Language	9
Common Rabbit Behaviours	12
Resting & Relaxing	14
Washing	17
Play	19
Investigation & Exploration	20
Vigilance	22
Fear	24
Feeding	26
Pooping	28
Digging	29
Marking	31
Social Interaction	32
Social Structure	34
Aggression	36
Reproduction	39
Abnormal Behaviour	40
Environmental Enrichment	42

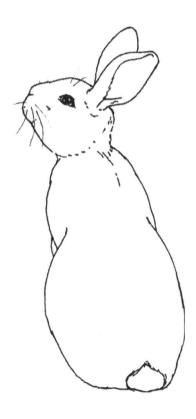

Introduction

Rabbits have a reputation for being cute and cuddly, but, underneath all that fluff, they are intelligent animals with complex behaviour and needs. You can learn a lot about your rabbit just by watching the way they behave. With the twist of an ear or the tilt of their head, rabbits can convey a wide range of emotions from happiness to aggression to fear. These subtle signals can give you an insight into what your rabbit is thinking and feeling, which in turn will help you to build a better relationship with your pet and provide for their needs.

Being able to tell whether your rabbit is happy or sad, angry or nervous is only the first step. If you really want to understand your rabbit better, you need to know what is making them feel that way. To understand the motivations behind a pet rabbit's behaviour, we need to put their behaviour and reactions into the context of the environment they evolved in. In comparison to cats and dogs, the domestication of rabbits is relatively recent. Selective breeding has superficially altered their appearance, but a rabbit's behaviour and needs are still shaped by the living conditions of their wild ancestors the European Rabbit (Oryctolagus cuniculus).

In the wild, rabbits live in social groups and build their homes in networks of underground tunnels called warrens. Rabbit society has a strict social structure and many of their social behaviours relate to deciding an individual's place in the hierarchy. Although rabbits are social within their family group, they are fiercely territorial towards outsiders and will aggressively defend their home. The protection of the warren and the benefits that come from group living are essential to a wild rabbit's survival. Rabbits are prey to a wide range of animals and this has a big impact on their behaviour and habits. The way rabbits live, feed, communicate, and move is all linked to minimising the risk of predation. Whatever activity a rabbit is engaged in, they must remain aware of their environment and ensure that their actions will not leave them exposed to potential threats.

The way of life of a wild rabbit may seem much removed from our pampered pets but much of the behaviour pets engage in is just wild rabbit behaviour adapted to their domestic environment. For example, a pet rabbit's obsession with chewing can be explained by the constant growth of their teeth to counter the wear caused by their natural diet of grass; their ability to hear a treat jar opening from two rooms away is down to acute senses developed to detect threats from predators. If your rabbit digs up your carpet or lawn, you can blame the wild rabbit's instincts to excavate underground passages for shelter. By putting your pet rabbit's behaviour in the context of the wild environment it evolved in, it is much easier to understand your rabbit's odd habits.

Recognising the influences of a rabbit's natural environment and instincts helps us to shape their environment to better support their behavioural needs. Rabbits that don't have the opportunity to express their natural behaviour patterns can end up bored and frustrated, and are more likely to be destructive and aggressive. Small changes, such as providing the opportunity to dig, places to hide, and even altering your feeding routine to suit the way rabbits graze can make a big difference to the health and happiness of your rabbit.

Body Language

Before you can identify and understand specific behaviours, it helps to have a basic grasp of rabbit body language. Body language is non-verbal communication such as facial expressions, movement of the limbs, posture (the way you sit or stand), and gait (the way you move). Humans use body language all the time, such as smiling when happy or having slumped shoulders when sad. Rabbits use body language, too, but their signals can be very different to humans and much more subtle. For example, when people are talking they usually maintain eye contact to signal they are paying attention to the conversation, where as a rabbit may listen whilst looking in the opposite direction with just an ear turned toward your voice.

The differences in body language between humans and rabbits, or even rabbits and other common pets, can make your rabbit's behaviour seem very puzzling or even frustrating. To understand your rabbit successfully you need to learn a completely new set of body language signals.

Ears

Rabbits' ears provide an excellent insight into how they are feeling. A slight change in ear direction can signal the difference between a curious rabbit and one ready to attack. When relaxed, rabbits' ears rest at approximately 45 degrees to the body, although a very relaxed/sleeping rabbit will lay its ears all the way back so they rest on its shoulders. Upright ears show a rabbit is alert and actively listening to its surroundings. A resting rabbit may raise one ear to an upright position to investigate movement or a noise. A curious rabbit will direct its ears forward, toward the object or sound it is investigating. An aggressive or nervous rabbit will fold its ears flat and point them back over its shoulders.

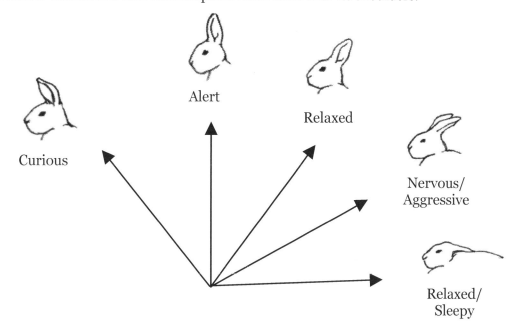

Alert

Relaxed

Curious

Nervous/
Aggressive

Relaxed/
Sleepy

Lop Ears

Unlike wild rabbits, not all pet rabbits have upright ears. There are several lop eared breeds with ears that hang down the sides of their head. It is also common to see crossbreeds whose ears fall somewhere in between - often fondly referred to as 'helicopter ears'. The amount of control these rabbits have over their ears varies greatly and it is more difficult to interpret the signals as any movement is often much more subtle.

In general, when relaxed lop eared rabbits carry their ears close to their head and pointing straight down. When curious or alert, a lop rabbit will rotate one or both ears forwards (so the inside of the earflap can be seen from the front) and may lift them or tilt their head to one side. Remember, ear movement when curious or alert is done to improve sound detection, so although the exact ear position may vary the goal of these movements is always to direct the ears towards a noise or potential noise.

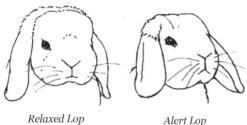

Helicopter Ears

Relaxed Lop   *Alert Lop*

A nervous or aggressive rabbit may be able to point their ears backwards similar to a rabbit with upright ears, but this requires more control and they may only manage to lift them slightly. Most lop eared rabbits cannot fold their ears as a nervous/aggressive rabbit with upright ears would.

If you have a lop eared rabbit, you'll need to learn your individual rabbit's signals by observing other body language clues and considering the context.

Whiskers

Whiskers are long stiff hairs found in the areas over the top lip and sides of the mouth. A few smaller ones also appear above and below the eyes. The nerves around the base of the whiskers are very sensitive, so sensitive in fact that they can detect changes in air currents.

Rabbits use their whiskers to assess their environment and this can give you clues about how they are feeling. When a rabbit is relaxed the whiskers rest pointing backward - when alert they stick out sideways or curve forward.

Rex breed rabbits only have short curly whiskers which aren't much help to your rabbit or your understanding of what it is thinking.

Nose

A rabbit's nose is much more sensitive to smell than a human's. You may have noticed your rabbit twitching its nose; this exposes more of the scent receptors improving smell detection - a bit like a human flaring their nostrils and taking a deep breath. Rabbits twitch their noses at varying rates depending how interested they are in the smells around them. A sleeping rabbit may barely twitch at all whereas a rabbit investigating a new object will twitch very rapidly. By watching how fast your rabbit is twitching his nose, you can tell how alert and interested in the surrounding environment he is.

Posture

A rabbit's posture, the way it sits or stands, is a big clue to what it might be thinking. An upright posture means your rabbit is alert and paying attention to the environment around him. A curious rabbit will lean forward to learn more, while a cautious one will lean away in case of danger. When scared, a rabbit will position its limbs ready to run or make itself small to avoid attracting attention. When being aggressive, it will try to make itself appear bigger so it seems more threatening. A very relaxed rabbit will lie down and stretch out its limbs.

Curious   *Alert*   *Relaxed*   *Nervous/Scared*

Locomotion

Many rabbit behaviours involve some form of movement. Behaviours like grazing, exploring, interacting with other rabbits, and marking all involve hopping. Pay attention to any deviation from your rabbit's normal hopping motion and speed. That will tell you how cautious or relaxed your rabbit is, and how urgent they feel it is to get where they are going. Rabbits hop faster when excited or running away, and slower when being cautious. When investigating something new, they slow right down to a 'walk', moving their back feet independently rather than hopping. A cautious or scared rabbit will also keep its body closer to the ground when moving.

Rabbits move in a hopping motion. Their front feet land 1-2, then the back feet hit the ground together and forward of the front feet. When going slowly the limbs remain tucked under the body.

As rabbits speed up their limbs fully extended forwards and backwards, so each hop carries them forward a greater distance.

Order of Steps: 1. First front foot 2. Secont front foot 3. Backfeet.

Rabbits flick their back feet out in an exaggerated manner as they hop away when they are annoyed, for example after being carried or let out of a carrier after a trip to the vet. If a rabbit gets wet feet it will flick them in a similar manner as it hops to remove the water.

Rabbits' powerful back legs allow them to jump several times their length, both vertically and horizontally; however wild rabbits generally only jump when fleeing a predator or occasionally as part of play. Pet rabbits are more likely to jump on and off things as part of exploration, which is important to keep in mind when designing secure accommodation.

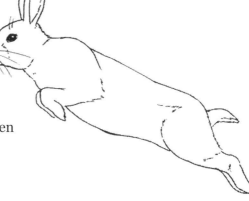

Common Rabbit Behaviours

Here are some of the most common rabbit behaviours. You can probably identify some of them from the tips on body language you've already read. Turn to the pages indicated to learn more about the motivations behind them and how you can adapt your rabbit's environment to accommodate them.

Resting (see pages 14-15)

Resting Stretched Out (see pages 15-16)

Scratching   *Licking Toes*   *Licking Body*   *Washing Ear*   *Scratching Ear*   *Washing Nose*

Grooming (see pages 17-18)

Begging
(see page 27)

Reaching Up
(see pages 20 & 26)

Standing Upright (Alert)
(see page 22-23)

Shake
(see pages 16 & 19)

Boxing
(see page 37)

Digging
(see pages 29, 39 & 41)

Stretching
(see page 16)

Collecting Bedding
(see page 39)

Stamping
(see page 23)

Eating
(see pages 26-27)

Eating Poop
(see page 28)

Pooping
(see pages 28 & 31)

Spraying
(see pages 31 & 39)

Rubbing Chin
(see page 31)

Resting in Groups
(see page 32)

Mutual Grooming
(see pages 32-33)

Mounting
(see pages 35 & 39)

Head Stretched Forward
-Requesting Grooming
(see pages 32-33)

Head Down Huddled
-Submissive
(see pages 34-35)

Meeting Rabbits
(see page 34-35)

Digging at Companion
(see page 30)

Nipping
(see page 33)

Circling
(see pages 37 & 39)

Charge
(see pages 35 & 37)

Fighting
(see pages 25 & 37)

Investigating
(see page 20)

Turning Away
(see page 24)

Crouching
(see page 24)

Hopping
(see page 11)

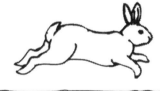
Running
(see pages 11, 19 & 24)

Chasing
(see pages 34 & 37)

Flicking Out Backfeet
(see pages 11 & 19)

Tail Wiggle
(see page 19)

Running Jumps
(see pages 19 & 24)

Jump
(see pages 11 & 19)

Resting & Relaxing

Rabbits are crepuscular, which means they are most active in twilight - the hours just before dawn and just after dusk. Most pet rabbits follow this pattern; however, some rabbits, particularly house rabbits, will make adjustments to accommodate their owner's routine. Altogether, rabbits spend about half of each day inactive, though it can seem like less because rabbits are light sleepers and have excellent hearing so it is rare to catch them with their eyes closed.

When a rabbit settles down at 'bedtime', which for a rabbit is usually from late morning to mid-afternoon, they usually choose a spot somewhere they can sleep for a few hours without being disturbed. In the wild, this would be the safety of the warren. For pet rabbits, it depends on the environment they live in. In a busy environment with lots of noises, smells, and visual stimuli, a sleeping box, tunnel, or behind your sofa may offer a safe place where they don't need to monitor their surroundings and can safely relax. In a quiet household, they may pick a more open area as there is less to watch out for.

Rabbits also rest for shorter periods on and off throughout the day and night. These 'naps' vary in location and duration as they are slotted in between other activities. For example a rabbit may settle down to wait next to the fridge near meal times or take time out to sunbathe whilst grazing. Because your rabbit is just taking a break, he is more alert to the environment around him and the place and position he chooses to lie down in will reflect this.

The position a rabbit chooses to rest in is a good way to judge how relaxed they are and how much attention they feel they need to be giving to their environment. As a prey species, being ready to run at the first hint of danger is an essential defence mechanism, so a rabbit will only lie down in a position that is slow to get up and flee from, if they feel the environment is safe and there will be no need to make a quick escape. However, being ready to get up does not necessarily mean your rabbit thinks there is imminent danger. Rabbits also remain alert for positive events such as the arrival of food and the activity of their companions (either rabbit or human).

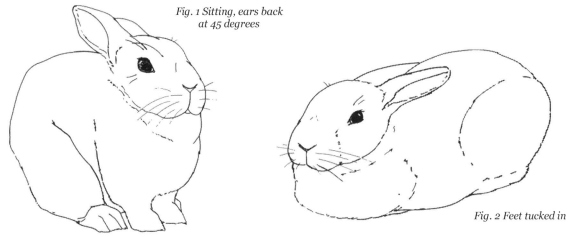

Fig. 1 Sitting, ears back at 45 degrees

Fig. 2 Feet tucked in

These illustrations show progressively more relaxed positions as the body lowers to the ground and limbs are more spread out. Rabbits often relax gradually, settling down further as time passes without anything that requires their attention or investigation.

Fig. 3 Front feet stretched forward (like the Sphinx)

Fig. 4 Back Feet Showing

Fig. 5 Legs to the Side

Fig. 6 Stretched out but still aware of environment.

Fig. 7 Lop rabbit fully stretched with head on floor.

Fig. 8 Asleep on side.

Fig. 9 Asleep on back with feet in the air and stomach visable.

Sleeping location and position can also reflect your rabbit's personality. A rabbit that normally has a nervous disposition is more likely to retreat to a secure covered area to relax than a laid back one, even when they share the same environment. A rabbit that is very curious about their environment and keen to interact with people may appear to relax less, as they are on the lookout for your arrival or new things to investigate.

The weather influences sleeping positions for rabbits living outside. In cold weather, a rabbit can conserve heat more efficiently with its limbs tucked in, so you are more likely to see your rabbit stretched out relaxing if the weather is warm or they live indoors.

Flopping Over

To get into a relaxed sleeping position, a rabbit will sometimes jump up and then fling themselves sideways or flop over, rolling to one side. It can be a bit alarming the first time you see this, as it looks more like your rabbit has had a sudden fit than decided to take a nap.

Waking Up

After a prolonged rest, rabbits stretch and yawn on waking. Before or after stretching a rabbit may also lift their front feet off the floor and shake like a wet dog. These behaviours all help your rabbit to wake up its muscles ready for action.

Stretching forward with the back legs extended and the chest forward over the front legs, the neck stretched forward, and the mouth open with the lips drawn back, showing the teeth.

Stretching backward with the hindquarters raised and the chest on the ground, and the front paws stretched forward with the toes spread.

Washing

Wild rabbits need to graze even in bad weather, and it is not unusual to see pet rabbits with access to outside space sitting out in the rain, even when they have access to shelter. The rabbit's thick fur coat allows it to do this whilst staying warm and dry.

A rabbit's fur contains two different types of hairs: a soft fluffy undercoat that keeps them warm in cold weather, protected by longer coarse hairs, called guard hairs. When a rabbit goes out in the rain, the guard hairs act like a raincoat shedding the water so the undercoat, and the skin underneath, stay warm and dry even when the surface of the fur gets wet.

To reveal the undercoat, blow gently into your rabbit's fur; it's often a different colour to the surface. In the wild a rabbit's fur also acts as camouflage. Each strand of fur is coloured in bands of black, brown, and grey to give the coat a speckled appearance. This helps rabbits to blend into their surroundings and hide from predators.

Rabbits have a vigorous grooming routine to keep their protective coat in good condition, licking, nibbling, and scratching at the fur to clean it.

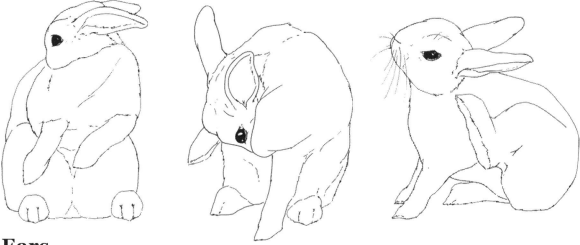

Ears

Rabbits find their long ears a bit difficult to reach, so they use a front paw to pull their ears down to rest along their cheek so they can wash the tips. They can then lick the ear as it curls under their chin. They scratch with a back paw to clean the inside of the ears.

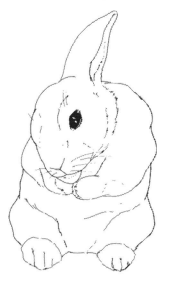

Face

Rabbits sit up to clean their faces. They prepare by lifting their front paws and giving them a couple of shakes to remove any dirt. They then lick their paws and, reaching up behind their whiskers, draw them forward repeatedly along the sides of their face.

Dirty or matted fur on a rabbit's front legs is a symptom of a possible respiratory infection as they wipe their noses on their paws. Rabbits with teeth problems may also have matted or wet fur around the chin, neck, or chest.

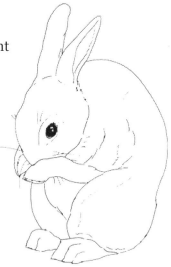

Feet

Rabbits do not have tough skin pads on the bottom of their paws like cats and dogs. Instead, fur protects and cushions the feet, so it is important they keep it in good condition and free from mats. To clean the fur rabbits stretch their back feet forward with the toes pointed upward, then stretch their head to the side to nibble and lick the paws. To clean more thoroughly they spread the toes to clean between them.

Rabbits with thin fur on the bottom of their feet, particularly Rex breeds, can suffer from sores on their heels. This can be made worse by excess weight, long nails, and hard flooring.

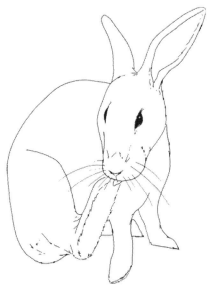

Play

Rabbits' favourite play activities are running and jumping games. A rabbit that is happy and full of energy may jump vertically, hop sideways, and put on bursts of speed interspersed with headshakes, twists, and mid-air kicks. Rabbit enthusiasts have dubbed this a 'binky'. Individual rabbits have their own routines. Some will be satisfied with the occasional jump, others elaborate twists and aerobatic displays.

Young, fit rabbits are most likely to engage in this behaviour, however, space is also an important factor. It is necessary both in that it encourages a rabbit to be happy enough to want to 'binky' and provides enough room to do so. Many rabbits perform 'binkies' just after being let out for exercise.

The movements rabbits display during play are similar to those they use to escape when frightened (see page 24); however, the direction of the jumps and twists is more random, and the bursts of speed shorter as they have no sense of urgency or specific destination to reach. Play is a form of learning and these behaviours probably originally evolved to help practice the skills rabbits use to escape predators, but they are also a fun way to burn off excess energy and express those moments where they are feeling so good they just have to jump for joy.

Rabbits also play with objects, particularly novel ones. They may nudge or pick up and throw or shake the toys. The play may begin as investigation but soon develops into a game as they shake and toss their toys. This makes play a fun way to keep your rabbit's mind stimulated and encourage exercise.

Investigation & Exploration

Rabbits are very curious creatures and quickly investigate any changes or new additions to their environment. The first sign that something has caught your rabbit's interest will be as he pauses and swivels his ears towards it while rapidly twitching his nose. If this initial auditory and olfactory assessment doesn't identify the object or detect danger, your rabbit will begin sneaking up to get a closer look.

When approaching an unidentified, and therefore potentially dangerous object, rabbits move a lot like a cat stalking prey. They stretch their body out, keeping low to the ground, and walk, instead of hopping, to avoid drawing attention. Once your rabbit reaches the object, he will stretch his head forward so he can sniff it without getting any closer than necessary. If anything startles him, such as sudden movement or noise, he will dart away and begin the process all over again.

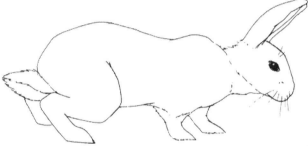

The rabbit's whole body posture is focused forward toward the object with the head stretched over the front feet and the ears stretched forward over the head.

If the object doesn't offer any apparent threat, a closer investigation is made and the object will be thoroughly sniffed, and may be nudged, shaken, tasted, or marked. The investigation may turn into play with the object being shaken and tossed around. Once your rabbit has investigated the object, if it has no value, e.g. a source of food, then he will quickly lose all interest in it – the fate of many toys.

Throughout the investigation process your rabbit is cataloguing the sounds, sights, and smells, and comparing them to his previous experiences. These experiences will affect how confidently he approaches the object. If the new object is similar to one he has previously experienced that he categorized as safe or 'good', then he will approach this similar object more confidently. Conversely, if it reminds him of a bad experience then more caution is used.

It is important for a rabbit to investigate their surroundings because it helps them to keep their knowledge of their territory updated so that they know where to find food, what places are safe and which to avoid, and what route to take if threatened by a predator. Rabbits have set paths they use to move through their territory, favouring routes that provide cover, e.g. the edge of a room or along a fence line. They will use a longer route over a shortcut that involves crossing an area of open ground, as this provides more protection from predators.

Wild rabbits have to adjust their territory and plan routes to accommodate natural obstacles like trees, tree roots, rocks, and water. By memorizing their territory and safe routes through it, rabbits can move faster if chased and are less likely to find themselves cornered by an unexpected obstacle. Pet rabbits can be fussy about the positioning of objects in their home, moving them out of the way of their preferred routes. Items that block passages such as wires are also 'removed' to keep the route clear.

The curious nature of rabbits can be a problem when trying to create a safe and secure environment. Not everything your rabbit may want to investigate, such as poisonous plants and electrical cables, will be safe for him. Blocking off areas often makes them more tempting to a curious rabbit, so ensure that barriers are rabbit-proof. A determined rabbit will jump, scrabble, climb, and push to get where it wants to go.

Socialisation

Your rabbit's innate curiosity can be a useful tool to aid socialisation, the process of learning to interact comfortably with people, and to make friends with a new rabbit. To your rabbit you are a very intriguing object to investigate, so if you sit very still and wait patiently your rabbit will come to investigate what you are doing. By allowing your rabbit to approach you in his own time, you give your rabbit control over the situation and how quickly they approach. Being able to sneak up gradually and run away if he wants to, makes the situation much less stressful than if you hold your rabbit or put him on your lap.

To begin, sit or lie on the floor in your rabbit's enclosure or an area he is comfortable exercising in. Being in familiar territory will make your rabbit more confident. Try not to move too much; if you need to scratch your nose make your movements slow and deliberate. The most important thing is to completely ignore your rabbit. Do not look at him or attempt to stroke or touch him. You may like to bring something else with you to focus on such as a magazine or book.

With patience, your rabbit's natural curiosity will compel him to investigate the "thing" in his territory. If your rabbit is nervous, you can increase the incentive to investigate you by placing food near you. When your rabbit approaches, continue to ignore him and let him investigate in his own time. This will teach your rabbit that coming near you does not mean you are going to make a move towards him. Your rabbit will also learn to form a positive association between being near you and receiving food. Rabbits like food so this is a compelling reason to spend more time in your company.

Once your rabbit has learnt that your presence is not a threat, you can start to teach him that interacting with you is a positive thing, too. You can use food treats again to provide the positive benefit. Later on, as your rabbit becomes more confident, the positive benefits will develop to include receiving social interaction and grooming.

This time hold the food in your hand, still ignoring your rabbit as he approaches. At first, your rabbit may run away after he takes the food but as he realises you are not going to chase him or try to steal the food back, he will stop retreating. If your rabbit is still nervous, you can try putting your hand flat on the floor next to the food to begin with. The idea is to get your rabbit used to having your hands in the area around him but not trying to touch or grab him.

As your rabbit gains confidence, touch him with one finger when he gets the treat. To begin with, he will move away again but he will soon learn this is not an indication of danger and start ignoring your touch. Increase the touching slowly until your rabbit is comfortable with being stroked and happy for you to touch him even when food is not available.

Vigilance

Rabbits are prey to a wide range of animals including foxes, cats, birds of prey, and stoats. This has a big impact on their behaviour and habits. Rabbits must constantly process information about their environment to detect potential threats and their bodies have evolved for this purpose with large ears to detect sound, sensitive noses, and vision that covers almost 360 degrees. In the wild, this enables them to spot possible predators quickly, giving them more time to escape. Pet rabbits also use the same techniques to monitor their environment for positive events, such as the arrival of their owner or food.

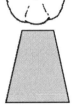

BLIND SPOT

When a rabbit is on alert their ears point straight up and their nose twitches rapidly to gather scent information. Rabbits' ears can rotate independently, which means you may see your rabbit direct one ear toward a noise and then swivel the other back and forth to listen for other sounds.

Rabbits' eyes are on the sides of their head, giving them a very wide field of vision. A rabbit can see in almost all directions apart from a blind spot right in front of its nose. This means your rabbit will not be looking at what is directly in front of its nose. Ear direction is a much better clue to what your rabbit is focusing its attention on.

To get a better view of potential threats, or owners bringing food, a rabbit will stand balanced on its back legs with its front paws held together against the chest in a begging position. For a quick glance around, instead of fully standing up, they just lift the front feet off the ground. Pet rabbits like high ground, such as an upturned box, to sit on to give them a good vantage point over their surroundings.

It's important that your rabbit's accommodation is tall enough for him to stand upright and look around, without hitting his head or ears on the enclosure roof. If a rabbit can check and reassure himself that an area is safe, he will feel more relaxed. If he cannot check for predators he must constantly worry that one may be sneaking up undetected.

Warning

Rabbits share look out duties; working as a team, they can monitor a wider area and are more likely to spot potential threats early. When an individual detects potential danger, it warns other members of the social group, whether human or rabbit, by stamping its back feet on the ground to make a single loud thump.

Rabbits also take cues from other rabbits' behaviour. If one rabbit in a group suddenly flees, other rabbits will follow even if they haven't personally detected danger. Unexpected sounds or movement quickly sends the whole group sprinting back to the warren for cover.

Rabbits also stamp to indicate annoyance, for example after being put in a carrier for a vet trip or picked up or returned to the cage after exercise. You will need to consider the context to decide why your rabbit thumped.

If your rabbit stamps frequently, try to work out what is causing the problem, perhaps a predator is near their enclosure or a strange noise is disturbing them. Your rabbit's senses are much more acute than humans, so you may not always be able to see or hear what is upsetting your rabbit. Make sure your rabbit has somewhere they feel safe to hide, plenty of activities to avoid frustration and if all else fails, use cardboard or padding under the cage/hutch to reduce the vibration and hence noise level.

Fear

Rabbits are naturally nervous animals because of their status as prey. Although a wild rabbit's main fear is predators, pet rabbits will react to other frightening experiences in the same way. Rabbits can come under attack from the ground or air. This makes them particularly wary of loud noises, sudden movement, and open spaces with no cover, as these can signal or increase the risk of an attack.

A frightened rabbit has three responses: freeze, flight, or fight. In extreme cases of terror, a rabbit will make a high-pitched scream. The response chosen by a rabbit will depend on the exact situation and the rabbit's past experiences. Rabbits can adapt their reaction to situations by learning from their previous experiences. For example if a rabbit learns that aggression (fight) is a successful way to escape a frightening situation, they will repeat that strategy when the situation next occurs.

Freeze

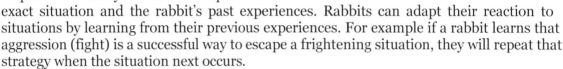

When freezing a rabbit will crouch, lowering its body and head, with its ears back, slightly folded and spread out to the sides. When a rabbit is very frightened it tenses making its eyes appear to bulge. The rabbit may also have one front paw in front of the other or be partially turned away ready to flee. Many predators rely on movement to identify prey and by making itself as small as possible and holding very still, the rabbit hopes to avoid detection.

Flight

Rabbits are sprinters rather than endurance runners. Their powerful back legs allow them to put on short bursts of speed so they can rapidly retreat to a warren when threatened. Rabbits' warren networks have multiple entrances to provide quick boltholes in an emergency. An escaping rabbit will avoid running in an easily followed straight line and instead dodge, weave, and backtrack, interspersed with jumps and zig-zags to avoid the predator.

If a pet rabbit is in a confined area, e.g. an exercise run or a room in your house, without somewhere to hide, they may panic and throw themselves at the walls trying to escape, jump a barrier they have not previously attempted or wedge themselves in to a small gap. This overwhelming urge to flee to safety can put them in more danger than the perceived threat, so to prevent injury it is very important that even the most relaxed rabbits always have access to somewhere to run to and hide.

Fight

If neither freezing nor running works and a rabbit is cornered, it will put up a fierce fight, twisting its body, and kicking out with its powerful back legs. Fear of interacting with humans can often show as aggression, as the rabbit attacks the scary hands, making them go away (see page 38).

Reducing Fear

Pet rabbits, like wild rabbits, feel more secure when they know there is a safe place nearby to hide in if they are frightened, but a rabbit's concept of what is safe cover is different to a human's. A rabbit can panic in a secure mesh run and feel safe in a cardboard box. They do not understand the concept of a mesh barrier being secure against predators. To a rabbit it feels like they are out in the open, whereas an enclosed box, even if it is just cardboard, provides the illusion of a safe hiding place. Having somewhere to hide will make your rabbit more relaxed in their home, even if they do not actually need to hide very often.

Rabbits that have had positive experience with a range of noises, places, and items will react less fearfully of new situations even if they have not encountered the exact situation before. If experience tells your rabbit that 99 percent of the time something new means something good, or at least not bad, your rabbit will be more confident when he encounters a situation outside his normal routine. A rabbit that has not experienced many novel objects or situations (so cannot predict whether something might be good or bad), or has experienced many negative or scary new things, will approach any new object or situation with extreme caution. Introduce new things to your rabbit slowly giving them the opportunity to explore in their own time and use rewards such as food to help them make positive associations with the new experience.

Many rabbits are nervous about being approached or handled by people. Again, a rabbit must learn from positive experiences that a human coming near them or touching them is not something scary. If a rabbit has not had adequate socialisation with humans, it will take time and patience (see page 21) for them to learn that interacting with you is not going to cause them harm. You can help make your rabbit feel more comfortable by altering the way you move when you are close by. Slow deliberate movements are much less likely to startle your rabbit and approaching from the side, where a rabbit's vision is best, will give him more time to recognise who or what is approaching. Try not to tower over your rabbit or present a dark silhouette against the light, like a swooping bird of prey. Talking in a calm quiet tone can also help your rabbit to anticipate and follow your movements, and allow him to identify you from other individuals.

Rabbits also take cues from their social companions. If one rabbit is relaxed about a situation, a nervous rabbit will consider the situation less threatening than if it was on its own. Therefore, a confident companion rabbit can help boost the confidence of a nervous rabbit.

Feeding

Rabbits are herbivores (plant eaters). In the wild, their main diet is grass although they also eat a range of other plants and supplement their diet with grain crops, twigs, and tree bark. These types of foods require different feeding behaviours such as stretching or digging to reach tender shoots and gnawing at tough tree bark. Alternative foods like tree bark are particularly important during winter when food is scarcer and rabbits may need to dig through snow or travel further from the warren to find enough grass.

Altogether wild rabbits spend around two-thirds of each day moving around their territory grazing and foraging. This is an important point to keep in mind as it means the types of food you feed, and the manner in which you feed them, can have a big impact on your rabbit's behaviour. If your pet rabbit doesn't have to spend time finding food, and it just arrives like clockwork in his bowl each day, then it leaves your rabbit with many spare hours when they have nothing to do. Without alternate activities to fill the hours that would usually be spent foraging, rabbits can quickly become bored; and with no appropriate outlet, natural feeding behaviours, such as striping bark from trees, can become destructive behaviours, like wallpaper stripping and cage chewing. The issue is often made worse by feeding an excess of commercial dry foods, which provide highly concentrated nutrition (packing lots of nutrients into a small volume of food), the exact opposite of a rabbit's natural diet (a high volume of low nutrient food). This further reduces the time a rabbit needs to spend eating and discourages natural browsing and foraging behaviours.

Providing a more natural feeding pattern will encourage your rabbit to exercise both its brain and body, helping to maintain a healthy weight and prevent boredom, as well as decreasing the likelihood of destructive behaviour such as chewing. Providing your rabbit free access to fresh grass or hay is essential to maintain good digestive function and helps mimic natural grazing. If you can provide secure access to grass, that is ideal, but that is not a practical option for everyone. You can still simulate grazing by growing grass from seed in a pot or tray or scattering cut grass* or hay around their pen. If your rabbit lives inside and you don't want hay scattered everywhere then just place it in several locations around your rabbit's home to encourage him to move about to seek out the tastiest pieces.

Rabbit's Teeth

Rabbits have two sets of teeth. The incisors, at the front, chop through grass and the molars, at the back of the mouth, to grind it up. Both sets of teeth grow continually throughout a rabbit's life. The wear caused by eating grass or hay is essential to prevent the teeth growing too long and cutting into the tongue and cheeks.

Incisors

Molars

---

*Grass should be cut with scissors, do not use lawn mower clippings; the heat and crushing action of mowing causes the grass to start fermenting which will upset the gut if eaten.

It's important that rabbits have an outlet for natural foraging behaviours as well as grazing. Rather than just putting food in a bowl, try to mimic some of the foraging a wild rabbit would do to find food. For example, you can hang up vegetables, so your rabbit has to stretch up to get them, as a wild rabbit might have to stretch up to reach the tender shoots from trees and bushes. You can also hide food in, under, or on top of objects (such as flowerpots, boxes, or paper bags) so your rabbit has to sniff it out then work out how to obtain it. Even simply scattering the food around the enclosure will give your rabbit more stimulation than a tidy pile in a bowl.

One way to feed dry food is using a 'treat' ball. This is a hollow ball with a small hole. You fill the ball with food and it falls out as your rabbit pushes the ball around the floor. You can usually find them for sale in the cat section of pet shops, or you can make your own from a box, cardboard tube, or bottle with holes cut in to let the food fall out. Encouraging your rabbit to move around to feed is a good way to increase their exercise and prevent obesity.

Begging

Rabbits are highly food motivated and will soon learn that you are the source of their meals. Some rabbits express excitement at meal times with grunts and circling their owner. Rabbits who receive food or treats by hand will 'beg' by standing on their back feet similar to the lookout position of an alert rabbit. Unlike an alert rabbit, when begging a rabbit points its ears either forward to detect the treat or backward as the nose is stretched up. The nose also tends to be higher in the air. Once a rabbit has learnt that this behaviour results in a treat it is often repeated.

Feeding your rabbit by hand is a good way to encourage interaction and develop a good relationship, but be careful you don't allow your rabbit to overindulge. Instead of feeding extra treats, reserve a portion of your rabbit's favourite mealtime foods to hand feed.

Pooping

Rabbits produce two types of droppings: hard round pellets (faecal pellets) and soft dark droppings (cecotropes), which they reingest.

Faecal Droppings

Faecal droppings are round balls, dark to light brown in colour, and fairly uniform in size. Rabbits usually deposit faecal droppings in a set latrine area but they can be scattered as part of territory marking. To aid with cleaning, you can train your rabbit to deposit the droppings in a litter tray. Begin by placing the tray in your rabbit's preferred toilet location and then place any droppings left outside the tray into it. It is most successful in neutered rabbits as they have less desire to mark their territory.

Cacography

The foods that make up a rabbit's natural diet are high in fibre but low in nutrients. To cope with this, rabbits have evolved a specialised digestive system that can ferment plant fibre to extract the additional nutrients locked inside (something that most animals, including humans, are not able to do). The nutrients extracted from the fermented fibre form into special droppings called cecotropes, which the rabbit produces and eats after they have returned to the warren (a process called cacography). In their new format, the digestive system can easily absorb the additional nutrients. Cecotropes are soft and dark brown, almost black, in colour; they are stuck together in a group that looks like a blackberry.

Whilst wild rabbits usually produce cecotropes at the same time each day, in pet rabbits it is dependent on their daily routine and feeding times. As rabbits collect and eat cecotropes directly from the anus as they produce them, you will never see them in a rabbit with a healthy digestive system. The only clue that your rabbit is producing them is seeing your rabbit duck its head down under its body and then sit up chewing.

Digging

Digging is an essential skill for wild rabbits; they dig networks of underground tunnels and chambers, called warrens, which provide them with shelter and protection from predators. Female rabbits complete most of the warren construction, but both male and female pet rabbits are avid diggers.

Rabbits dig with their front feet, scraping soil under their body and out between their back legs. As the tunnel lengthens, they will back out of the passage, drawing the soil out with them. They spread out the mounds of excavated soil with forward pushes of their front feet to stop it building up around the tunnel entrance.

If your rabbit has access to an outdoor run on soil you may need to bury mesh under the soil to limit the extent of the excavation and prevent escapes. The mesh can be placed on top of the grass to prevent digging completely, under the grass (lift the turf and re-lay over the mesh) to allow shallow digging, or buried to form an underground mesh box to prevent escape whilst still allowing short tunnels.

Tunnelling behaviour in rabbits kept indoors is not always as obvious; it may just seem like general destructive behaviour. Rabbits often try to extend existing shelter, for example extending the 'tunnel' between a sofa and the wall by chewing and digging into the sofa (it being the less solid option than the floor or wall). The corners of rooms are another spot that many rabbits view as ideal potential tunnel entrances.

Many owners find digging undesirable behaviour because their pet rabbit's environment is unsuited to it. Whilst these behaviours are fine in a natural environment, when the environment your rabbit is manipulating with its teeth and claws includes your wallpaper, furniture, or lawn, it can seem very destructive.

You are unlikely to succeed if you try to stop your rabbit digging completely. Remember this is perfectly natural behaviour for a rabbit. Instead, you need to redirect the behaviour to a more appropriate outlet by providing opportunities for them to engage in digging without causing damage. If you don't, your rabbit will dig anyway, even if this means chewing its way through your carpet in the process.

You can provide a digging area using a storage box, wooden crate, or child's sandpit filled with suitable digging material. As well as soil, boxes can be filled with shredded paper, hay, dried leaves (from rabbit-safe trees), snow, or any other suitable material.

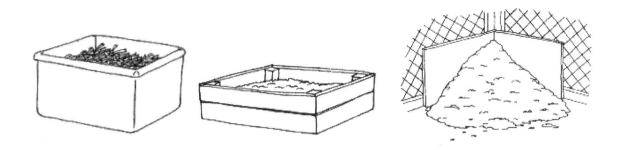

As a rabbit's main purpose for digging is to create tunnels, a pre-made tunnel system of cardboard boxes or plastic piping will also reduce your rabbit's urge to dig their own tunnels.

Other Digging

Rabbits don't just dig to create tunnels. Digging, along with chewing, is one of the most effective tools a rabbit has to manipulate their environment. Without paws that are able to grip objects, rabbits use digging as a way to move things out of their way, clear a spot to rest, or unearth food. A rabbit will also dig at a rabbit or human to indicate the want them to move and to express anger or frustration. You'll need to consider the context of your rabbit's digging to work out his purpose.

Digging without a purpose, i.e. constant repetitive scratching at the same spot, is abnormal behaviour, a sign of a rabbit that is suffering from boredom and frustration (see page 40) and their environment needs adjusting to better meet their behavioural needs.

Marking

Rabbits mark territory and objects that belong to them with pheromones secreted from scent glands located under their chin and next to their anus. This smelly messaging system lets other rabbits know who they are and where their territory is, helping rivals avoid each other (preventing unnecessary fights) and allowing potential partners to find each other during the mating season. It also helps a rabbit identify its own territory, making it feel more secure. Unfortunately, human noses lack the level of sensitive scent receptors needed to interpret exactly what these messages say, but, in simple terms, it means, "this is mine".

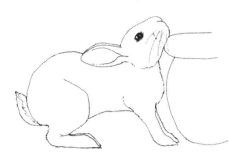

Chinning

To deposit scent from the gland located under the chin, rabbits rub the underside of their chin over objects. Rabbits often mark new objects in their environment this way. When more than one pet rabbit has access to an area, it is common to see one rabbit following another around chinning objects after the first to remark them. As well as objects, rabbits sometimes mark their owners in the same way.

Spraying & Droppings

The scent glands next to their anus add scent to rabbit's droppings and urine. The droppings are scattered over the territory and left in piles at important markers or high points.

Male rabbits also use urine to scent mark. To cover a wide area the rabbit stands on its front legs and jumps/twists to raise the back legs from the floor and squirts urine. Male rabbits also spray females during courtship and other males during fights to indicate dominance over them.

Influences on Marking

Rabbits usually begin to mark at sexual maturity, but in pet rabbits that are kept singly, the lack of scent from other rabbits can delay it. A change in season, territory, or the scent of other rabbits or animals can suddenly trigger marking behaviour.

Rabbits increase their marking frequency when other rabbits are present. Scent is important to rabbits and marking their territory helps them to feel more secure. Introducing a new rabbit usually corresponds with an increase in marking, even in neutered rabbits, gradually decreasing again as the new rabbit integrates with the group. Rabbits will also mark more when they move to new territory, such as getting a new cage.

Although both male and female rabbits mark their territory, it is usually the dominant male's role in a group to mark the group's territorial boundaries, so in general, males mark more frequently than females. Males are also more likely to use spraying to mark than females.

Neutering is the most reliable way to stop undesirable scent marking with both urine and faeces. After the operation your rabbit's hormone levels will decrease, and along with them the urge to mark their territory.

Social Interaction

Watching two companion rabbits together is fascinating; they sit, play, eat, and groom together, and seek reassurance from their companion when worried. When not in direct contact with each other they will usually be within eyesight, following each other from room to room or from hutch to run.

Having a companion of the same species allows them to engage in a range of behaviours that is not always possible, even with the best of human friends. Rabbit's complicated language of body signals is very different from humans and other animals. Having a companion to relate to that 'speaks' the same language means they can have much more rewarding social interactions.

Another rabbit is one of the best ways to enrich your rabbit's life. The difference in behaviour once a second rabbit is introduced can be remarkable. Rabbits kept with companions are generally more active and interested in their environment. They are also less prone to abnormal behaviour caused by stress and boredom. You may also find they are more interested in toys, as seeing a companion with a toy always makes it more desirable.

Resting Together

Rabbits living in social groups often spend rest periods in physical contact with each other. This helps reinforce their social bonds as well as share body heat.

 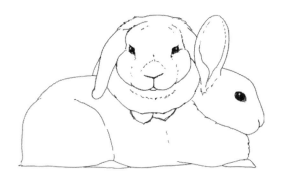

Social Grooming

Mutual grooming is a popular activity for rabbits living in groups. This helps keep areas clean that are hard for an individual rabbit to reach, such as the head and ears. Grooming is also a social activity helping to form and maintain bonds. When you introduce a new rabbit, grooming is often the first sign of their acceptance in to the social group.

Rabbits request grooming from each other by extending their head forward low to the ground or pushing their head under the chin of the other rabbit. Pet rabbits demand grooming from their owners in the same way. You can ask for grooming by placing your hand on the ground in front of your rabbit, but try not to be offended if your rabbit ignores the request.

There is a social etiquette to grooming. If a rabbit high up the social ladder asks for grooming, any well mannered lower ranked rabbit will oblige. If they ignore the request then the other rabbit may express their displeasure with a quick nip or even digging at the other rabbit to get attention. Conversely, it is a bit rude for the underdog to demand grooming from his superiors and they may totally ignore any such requests. The grooming etiquette is often not as strict when there are only two or three neutered rabbits living together. Most pairs are quite relaxed and will take it in turns to groom each other, even if it's just the odd lick.

Whether your rabbit grooms you or not, grooming or stroking your rabbit is an important part of forming a relationship and socialising with your rabbit. If you are your rabbit's only social companion, it is even more important. Rabbits prefer to be stroked on the forehead, cheeks, ears, and along the spine but you will need to experiment to learn your rabbit's preferences. Getting your rabbit used to being touched is essential if you want to be able to pick up your rabbit and to perform tasks such as health checks, nail trimming, and coat maintenance.

Preferred areas for stroking/grooming.

Areas to acclimatise rabbits to touching for picking up.

Areas to acclimatise rabbits to touching for health checks/nail clipping.

Nip & Nudge

Nipping is a form of communication, and is not always related to aggression. Rabbits nudge, or head butt, to gain attention or ask for grooming. If your rabbit fails to get the attention it wants then it may accompany the next nudge with a nip.

Nipping, when not accompanied by other aggressive behaviours, is generally a sign of annoyance; something is not going the way your rabbit would like. A nip can mean: get out of my way, stop doing that, or why aren't you doing what I want, for example... "Why [nip] have you stopped grooming my head?"

Rabbits use this form of 'communication' with humans as well as other rabbits. Nipping does not usually break the skin; it is more like a pinch. It is more painful on bare human skin than it would be to a rabbit cushioned with fur, which can make it seem more aggressive than intended. It can become an issue if your rabbit learns that nipping generates the desired response, so try to avoid reacting in a way that furthers your rabbit's goal.

Social Structure

Within a social group rabbits form separate male and female hierarchies, sometimes called pecking orders. A high position in the female hierarchy gives the choice of best grazing and nesting sites, and the top position in the male hierarchy gives control over breeding females and responsibility for the marking and defence of the group's territory against rival groups.

The hierarchy is not a fixed structure; as the rabbits that make up the group change, so does the position of each rabbit. The main trigger for a change in the social hierarchy is young rabbits reaching sexual maturity. However, anything that has the potential to affect a rabbit's position in the hierarchy can trigger a reshuffle. This can include rabbits joining or leaving the group, young rabbits reaching sexual maturity, illness or injury, or a change in resource availability.

The social groups of pet rabbits are usually more stable as the group's members and territory are less subject to change. Neutering helps to mitigate the desire for competition and is particularly important to prevent disputes between young rabbits reaching sexual maturity. However, there are still factors that have the potential to cause an upset in the hierarchy. These include: a rabbit added, removed, or temporarily separated from the group; the smell of another rabbit in the area; a trip to the vet causing one rabbit to smell different; an illness or injury to one of the group's members; or, a new or changed territory (new housing).

Forming the Hierarchy

Rabbits use a variety of behaviours, including posturing, chasing, and mounting to confirm their rank in comparison to other group members. Similar behaviours are displayed between pet rabbits when new rabbits are introduced.

Assessing

When rabbits are unsure about their position in the hierarchy or there is no clear top rabbit then they approach each other cautiously. They will first size each other up. Often rabbits will groom or graze apparently oblivious to each other's presence. Despite appearances, they are actually paying close attention, waiting to see what the other rabbit will do and deciding on their own response. Neither rabbit is keen to express dominance or risk aggravating the other rabbit by being too forward. As they become more confident that the lack of action means the other rabbit is not posing a threat, they will begin to interact.

Neither rabbit is looking at the other, but they are both aware of each others presence and trying to decide what to do about it!

Submission

When approached by a dominant rabbit, a subordinate rabbit may adopt a submissive posture, with his head down and his body crouched, to make himself appear small and unthreatening. This position is similar to a rabbit asking for grooming, but the head and neck are not stretched forward.

Crouching down makes a rabbit appear unthreatening and signals they have no desire to challenge the other rabbit.

Chasing

If the dominant rabbit is still not satisfied he may encourage the other rabbit to move away by chasing him or her. Chasing exerts the dominance of the chasing rabbit, and giving way when chased shows acceptance by the lower ranking rabbit. If a nervous rabbit is slow to move, the dominant male may dig at the ground or the rabbit's fur to encourage him to move out the way, or nip and then chase him. The fleeing subordinate will move low to the ground and the dominant will have his body and tail raised to appear larger. Chases are usually short dashes and the dominant rabbit may wander off in between and repeat the chase only when the subordinate draws attention by moving or getting too close. If the ranking is unclear and the rabbits attempt to chase each other, it may develop into a fight.

Chasing and mounting is used to demonstrate dominance over other rabbits.

Mounting

Chasing is often interspersed with mounting. Both male and female rabbits, including those neutered, also use mounting to establish and demonstrate dominance in the social hierarchy. It is particularly common when new rabbits are first introduced and becomes less frequent once the hierarchy is established. The dominant rabbit mounts the other rabbit, often from the side or head.

Fight

When rabbits cannot settle the hierarchy, or a rabbit wants to challenge for the dominant position, the disputes can escalate into aggression (see page 37). Physical fights between rival rabbits are a last resort as any injury could leave a rabbit vulnerable to predators. Sometimes mounting/chasing can look quite aggressive but it should not leave wounds. If your rabbits are causing injuries to each other they need to be separated.

Introducing Rabbits

Rabbits benefit greatly from living in a social group but the introductions must be done carefully. If you have not introduced two rabbits before then consult an expert for advice before going ahead. The best matches are those that take into account rabbits' natural social structure. As rabbits of the same sex are naturally competitive, matches between a neutered male and female are easiest to make. Two unneutered males are the most likely combination to fight and male siblings should be neutered prior to sexual maturity if they are to be kept together, to minimise the risk of hierarchy disputes. Any introductions must be done in a neutral area to avoid territory disputes (see page 36).

Aggression

Rabbits have a reputation for being cute and cuddly, but when it comes to defending themselves or their territory, they can attack viciously. There are several reasons for rabbits to display aggression and it is not always immediately obvious what the cause is; it is also possible for there to be several contributing factors.

Any time your rabbit displays aggression that is out of character you should book a check up with a vet to rule out pain or illness making them lash out, before considering behavioural causes.

Territorial Aggression

Most rabbit aggression relates to territorial disputes. In the wild, each group of rabbits is headed by a dominant male. He defends the group's territory against rival males by marking and patrolling the group's grazing areas and the boundaries between groups' territories.

Aggression that corresponds with the onset of sexual maturity (between 4-12 months), or with the introduction of a new rabbit, is usually territory related. The limited size, fixed boundaries, and lack of rival groups in a domestic setting means that the whole area a pet rabbit has access to becomes its territory. If you place a new rabbit in to this area, it will have, in effect, arrived unannounced in the centre of occupied territory. A rabbit's natural reaction to this unexpected invasion is to attack aggressively to force the invader out. The 'invader's' inability to move away (an indication of submission or lack of challenge) and exit the territory only heightens the occupying rabbit's aggression. A dominant male may also direct aggression at existing companions that challenge his position, for example a young male reaching sexual maturity.

As this aggression relates to defending their home, it is usually limited to when a rabbit is in its own territory. If the aggression disappears when the rabbit is in a neutral location, this is a strong indication of territorial aggression. You should use a neutral location routinely when introducing rabbits to minimise the risk of this type of aggression.

Male territorial aggression is usually only targeted at other male rabbits; however, when a rabbit is unable to reach the target of its aggression, for example, a rabbit in an adjacent enclosure, they may displace aggressive behaviour on to other rabbits within their enclosure. It's very rare for a male rabbit to show territorial aggression towards human 'invaders', however if you handle another rabbit, accidentally transferring their scent to your hands and clothes, this may confuse your rabbit into targeting you by mistake.

Posturing

Most disputes between rabbits begin with posturing, chasing, and vocalisations (grunting and growling). An aggressive rabbit will stand on its toes, ready to move and making itself look larger. It will carry its tail up, and its ears folded and pointed backward. Rabbits also signal aggressive intent with short charges at the other rabbit, growling, digging at the ground, or pacing back and forth.

The aim of these behaviours is to intimidate the opponent into backing down without the need for a physical altercation. Avoiding a fight lowers the risk of receiving an injury that could compromise a wild rabbit's ability to function, and therefore survive.

Chase

Rabbits use chasing to exert their dominance. Most disputes involve chasing to some extent and most end with the winner chasing away the loser. You can identify aggressive chasing from other reasons for chasing (such as courtship, play, hierarchy disputes) by the speed and attitude of the chaser. When chasing with aggressive intensions, a rabbit will move rapidly and directly at their opponent with their head down and ears back.

The chase ends when the winner is satisfied the loser has left their territory. Limited space in a pet rabbit's enclosure can prolong aggression, as the loser cannot move far enough away to satisfy the winner. When there isn't a clear winner, chasing can turn into rapid circling which escalates into a fight.

Fight

Fights between rabbits begin with intense chasing as the rabbits circle, jump, and lunge at each other, attempting to bite their opponent. When they manage to latch on with their teeth, they roll across the ground biting and kicking at each others stomachs with their powerful back feet. The fight ends when one opponent backs down and flees, chased by the winner. Fights often result in torn ears and bite wounds to the nose, shoulders, hips, and groin. The most serious fights happen between unneutered males.

Some of the behaviours shown during territorial aggression are similar to those in hierarchy disputes, and in both cases the rabbits are attempting to win clear dominance over each other. However, when the dispute is over territory, the end goal is to expel the loser rather than integrate them into the group. The stakes are much higher so the interactions are high paced; the defending rabbit wants to head off potential rivals quickly and dissuade future challenges.

Female Territorial Aggression

Whilst male rabbits are the most active in defending their territory, females will aggressively defend their nest sites and the immediate area around the warren. In domestic rabbits, this usually translates to the cage or hutch, particularly the sleeping area and food bowls.

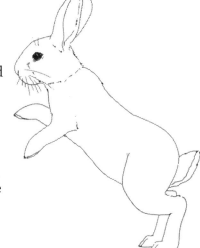

A defensive female will be aggressive towards males and other females, but in pet rabbits this behaviour is most often displayed as aggression towards their owner when they place their hands in the hutch or cage.

The rabbit will lunge and rear up on her hindquarters to attack at the intruder with her front paws. She will tense her paws with the digits spread to give the nails maximum impact; it can be a single downward strike or repeated strikes in a mid-air boxing motion. Female rabbits are particularly vocal, grunting and growling when attacking. They may make short charges to encourage the invader to leave but are less likely to engage in long chases and fights than males.

Reducing Territorial Aggression

Neutering reduces both territorial and hierarchy-related aggression by removing the hormones driving the competitive urge. It is usually very successful at resolving female territorial aggression directed at humans.

If you plan to house male rabbits together then you must have them neutered before sexual maturity when the urge to fight over territory develops and closely watch for the signs of disputes. Some males are particularly territorial even after neutering and will not tolerate another male in their enclosure. Rabbits have good memories and may remember previous disagreements with individual rabbits and react to them aggressively even after neutering; for example, once two males have fought and been separated, they will often continue to fight if introduced again.

Fear Aggression

Aggression is not always a sign of a rabbit exerting its dominance. Rabbits that are fearful of other rabbits or humans may use aggression to prevent interactions they find frightening. The rabbit learns that if they display aggression towards the rabbit (or human) they are frightened of, they will go away. For example, if they growl when you put your hand in their cage you will avoid doing that in future. Once they have learnt that aggression is a successful strategy, they repeat the behaviour in future to pre-empt attempts at interaction.

As the rabbit is trying to defend itself, rather than its territory, it will only show aggression when it is feeling cornered (e.g. confined to a cage), otherwise normal fearful behaviour such as avoidance is shown (see page 24). A nervous rabbit will usually begin with a warning growl and attack with a short lunge if directly approached; it will not chase away the invader or want to engage in a fight.

Fear aggression is a result of a lack of socialisation or negative past experiences. As rabbits' experiences with humans and other rabbits may be different, they will not necessarily be fear aggressive towards both. To reduce the aggression you need to address the underlying fear by creating new, positive associations with interactions, such as offering your rabbit treats when it approaches you.

Reproduction

Rabbits are prolific breeders, and without the restrictions of living in the wild, pet rabbits will breed all year. Rabbits can breed from 10-12 weeks, and a female can produce a litter every four weeks, although allowing her to do so has serious consequences for her health and that of the babies.

Courtship

During courtship, the male chases the female. Unlike aggressive chasing courtship is much more relaxed and much slower paced – where there is space the male may follow some distance from the female. As the male closes in, he circles the female with his tail held high and sprays her with urine to mark her with his scent. Actual mating is very brief, with the male mounting the female for only a few seconds.

In a domestic setting, courtship behaviour can be transfered on to human companions. Unneutered male rabbits may circle their owner's legs and spray them with urine, in an imitation of courtship. Rabbits can be quite vocal during this display making grunts, growls, and honking sounds.

Nesting

A few days before giving birth, a female rabbit collects bedding material, such as dry grass, to build a nest. She will select individual pieces, filling her mouth and then visiting the nest site to deposit it. The female then lines the nest with fur, which she plucks from her stomach and dewlap (the fold of skin under her chin), to keep the babies warm.

After giving birth, the female only visits the nest for a few minutes once or twice a day to feed the babies, often in the middle of the night. When she leaves the nest she seals the entrance with loose soil to deter predators. The babies develop rapidly and by three weeks will be leaving the nest to feed on grass.

Female rabbits can have phantom pregnancies during which they go through the motions of building a nest but are not pregnant. You can prevent phantom pregnancies by having your rabbit spayed.

Neutering

Many pet rabbits are neutered which allows them to enjoy the companionship of other rabbits without the risk of pregnancy. If left unneutered a single male-female pair could be responsible for hundreds of offspring in just a single year.

Unneutered rabbits, even when not bred, often display behaviour associated with reproduction. Neutering pet rabbits is advisable to prevent frustration, anti-social behaviour like spraying, marking, and territorial aggression, as well as to prevent accidental breeding.

Abnormal Behaviour

One of the benefits of being able to recognise your rabbit's normal behaviour is that you can then quickly identify behaviour that is out of character. Your rabbit's behaviour reflects how they are feeling, so changes from normal behaviour can signal a problem that needs addressing.

Illness

As rabbits are prey animals, they hide signs of illness to avoid catching the attention of predators. Even in a domestic setting rabbits will often show very little outward signs of being unwell until they are very sick. Often the first hint of potential illness is the feeling of "something not being quite right" with your rabbit's behaviour. For example, they may be slower to come and greet you, less excited about food or spend less time engaged in play activities. Knowing your rabbit's normal behaviour and routine will help you spot these subtle changes in behaviour that may indicate your rabbit is unwell.

Some common changes from normal behaviour include:

Alertness: Being less active than normal and reluctant to move about and engage in normal activities.

Resting: Being restless and unable to find a comfortable position to sit or lie in. Sitting huddled up. Rabbits that are in pain may also grind their teeth harshly. A gentler purring sound made with the teeth is the opposite - a sign of pleasure.

Eating: A change in eating habits including eating less or not at all, drooling, or a change in food preferences, e.g. only eating favourite foods or soft foods.

Toileting: A change in toileting e.g. losing litter training, producing less or no droppings, or having diarrhoea. A rabbit's digestive system is very sensitive and a change in droppings is often the first indication of illness.

Grooming: As rabbits are usually very clean animals, soiled or dirty fur may indicate illness. Excessive scratching or plucking fur, other than for nest building, can also indicate a behaviour or health issue. Excessive scratching or head shaking are symptoms of ear mites and should be checked by a vet.

Movement: A change in normal motion e.g. limping, stumbling, weakness of the hind limbs, or lack of coordination. Holding the head in an abnormal position e.g. tilted to one side.

If your rabbit exhibits any of these or other changes from their normal behaviour, you should contact your vet promptly for advice.

Boredom

Another common cause for abnormal behaviour is the stress caused by boredom and frustration. A wild rabbit has an ever changing environment and something to do all day from digging its home to looking for food and interacting with other animals. In comparison, a pet rabbit's environment can be very static; they may be in the same pen for months or years with very little change. Often their food, bed, and litter tray are so close together they only have to take a few hops to have all their basic needs met. It may sound like a life of relaxed luxury but without any activities to occupy themselves rabbits quickly become bored, and this has serious consequences for their mental and physical well-being.

As boredom is often an on-going problem, some of the behaviours associated with it may have become routine for your rabbit. Unlike illness, which is characterised by a sudden change from your individual rabbit's normal behaviour, boredom is often characterised by normal behaviours that are taken to an extreme or displayed in an unusual context. For example:

- Repetitive behaviour such as over grooming, rattling or chewing the cage bars, excessive digging or pacing. Often these were originally normal behaviours, but they have become compulsive and can become so extreme that rabbits will injure themselves performing them.

- Destructive behaviour, such as eating the enclosure, chewing wallpaper, or destroying their owner's belongings. When you don't provide enough suitable activities for your rabbit, he will create his own fun and this often involves property destruction.

- Instead of hyper-focus on an activity, rabbits can also display the opposite, becoming apathetic and spending all their time resting in one position, and not interacting with their environment.

Environmental Enrichment

To prevent boredom, you need to create an environment that provides activities to occupy your rabbit, a process called environmental enrichment. An enriched environment should encourage and provide an outlet for natural behaviour like digging, foraging, and socialising; encourage physical activity and generally give your rabbit something to do with their spare time. The result should be a happier, fitter, and more well balanced rabbit.

Environmental enrichment is not difficult or expensive. Anything that makes your rabbit think or interact with their environment is a form of enrichment. When you talk to your rabbit or clean out his pen, you provide new sounds and scents, social interaction, and curious behaviour that requires thought and investigation – this is enrichment. Even a simple object like a brick from your garden can temporarily enrich your rabbit's environment; it will provide new smells, and the opportunity to display natural behaviours like scent marking and jumping.

Here are some ideas:

Hiding Places

Creating hiding places from items such as a covered cat litter box, cardboard box, storage crate, or by laying a dustbin on its side. These have that added benefit of providing something to sit on top of.

Give your rabbit a choice of shelters. Your rabbit may not want to retreat to a completely enclosed box so include areas that are only semi-sheltered. In summer, these provide shade and in the winter, some protection from bad weather. Experiment with different materials to provide see-through sections or windows.

Tunnels are popular with rabbits and are easy to make. You can use cardboard or plastic tubes, rectangular boxes, a towel draped over a line of string, or a row of foot stools. You can combine boxes and tunnels to make an artificial warren.

Ground Cover

Different surfaces encourage different behaviours. A layer of straw can encourage digging and foraging behaviours, particularly when combined with hidden food. Mats made from natural fibres such as sisal can be chewed and dug at. Rabbits enjoy a cool area such a bare earth, tile, or paving to stretch out on when it is hot. If your rabbit does not have access to soil or grass it can be provided by using a large shallow tray such as an under bed storage box. Rabbits are often more cautious when moving on slick surfaces like linoleum or wood, so a rug can encourage your rabbit to explore further and move faster.

A Variety of Levels

Give your rabbit a range of levels from just a few inches upwards. They enjoy climbing and jumping on top of things, and the higher vantage point gives them more to see. You could use an upturned tray or storage box, step stool, low table, tree stump, or build your rabbit a shelf. If your rabbit is outside, why not create a natural mound of soil instead of having a perfectly level floor?

Obstacles

Create obstacles for your rabbit to navigate or remove. A low horizontal stick or line of bricks provides something to jump over. A row of sticks planted upright or hanging down can create a barrier that your rabbit can shape for themselves. If your rabbit can see its entire enclosure

Indoors

Outdoors

from every point, then it has no need to visit the far end. Try introducing large items that your rabbit has to explore behind or small partitions.

Novel Objects

Any new object provides the opportunity for scent marking (rubbing with chin), sniffing, and investigation even if it provides no further entertainment. Many household items, such as boxes, cardboard tubes, flowerpots, or a baby rattle can be converted into rabbit toys. You can make old toys more interesting again by changing their smell. Use natural non-toxic scents or food flavourings like lemon or peppermint. Herbs are also a good source of scent and can be hidden for your rabbit to hunt out and eat.

Sound

Rabbits have good hearing and whilst you do not want to frighten your rabbit, sound provides another form of stimulation. You can use the radio; try classical music or talk shows rather than music with a thumping beat, or use CDs of 'natural' sounds like bird song. This will help your rabbit become accustomed to a range of human voices and sounds, so they are likely to be more relaxed about unusual noises such as fireworks. If you rabbit is used to a very quiet environment any unusual noises will seem more threatening, so start new noises at a low volume and turn the sound up gradually. Don't feel silly talking to your rabbit, either. Although rabbits don't naturally use speech as communication they can learn to recognise your voice and tone even if they don't understand exactly what you are saying.

More Enrichment Tips

Do not provide every form of enrichment at once or fill your rabbit's enclosure up with so many items they have no room left to run and jump. Once an object has been investigated, if it does not have any value, such as being a source of food or a hiding place, it will quickly be ignored, so it is important to rotate the toys you provide for your rabbit to give it new things to investigate.

It is important that you stimulate your rabbit mentally as well as physically by providing new challenges that encourage them to work out problems, such as how to find food. If an activity becomes routine it will provide little mental stimulation even if it is physically challenging.

Give your rabbit a range of enrichment opportunities and observe them to see which types encourage investigation and activity and which are ignored. If your rabbit does not play with the items you provide, then you need to provide items that are more interesting. A brightly coloured carrot shape chew may look exciting to you but if it smells and tastes just like the other pieces of wood in your rabbit's environment, it will pay it no more attention than it does them. To encourage your rabbit to be more active you need to give it a reason to interact with its environment. Consider ways to develop activities they enjoy and change activities they do not to make them more fun.

Some forms of enrichment are more appropriate for particular rabbits and housing set ups than others. You will need to tailor things to your individual rabbit's physical capabilities. Choose items that suit your rabbit; a nervous rabbit may enjoy enrichment that provides more places to hide, an active one, things to climb. Remember your rabbit will learn new things so a nervous rabbit may become more confident once it has hiding places and then enjoy other activities. Do not overwhelm your rabbit with too many changes at once.

Safety

Enriching your rabbit's environment does come with an element of risk. Just like if you give a child bike to ride, you risk them falling off! The same principle applies to rabbits. Providing an empty environment minimises the risks of physical injury but it can have serious implications on their mental well-being. A rabbit with nothing to do quickly becomes bored and can exhibit a range of abnormal behaviour. They are also more likely to suffer from physical problems such as muscle wastage and obesity. So, a rabbit owner must do what every parent does – minimise the risks whilst still providing a stimulating environment.

Check toys and the enclosure regularly for damage and sharp edges. All toys should be safe to chew and not of a size that could slip around a neck or foot and get stuck. Make certain that any items that may be unsafe for your rabbit to investigate, such as poisonous plants or electrical wires, are inaccessible.

Conclusion

By now you should be feeling familiar with many of your rabbit's habits, and beginning to understand why he does what he does.

Keep in mind that many factors influence your rabbit's behaviour, and their excellent senses mean sometimes they may be reacting to something we cannot see, hear, or smell. It will take time for you to hone your observational skills and become familiar with your rabbit's individual quirks and how he interacts with the environment around him. Although understanding rabbit's habits isn't always easy, it can have big rewards for both you and your bunny.

By understanding the motives behind your rabbit's behaviour, you can provide an environment in which your rabbit can safely thrive. Knowing how to interpret a rabbit's body language will lead to a stronger bond and enriched life for your pet, and a more harmonious household.

Further Reading

Why Does My Rabbit ...? by Anne McBride

The Relaxed Rabbit: Massage for Your Pet Bunny by Chandra Beal

How to Have a Relaxed Rabbit by Emma Magnus

The Problem with Rabbits by Pat Rees

Living with a House Rabbit by Dr Linda Dykes & Helen Flack

Greenfoods for Rabbits and Cavies by F.R. Bell

Bonding Rabbits by Fiona Campbell

Useful Organisations

Rabbit Welfare Association & Fund
PO Box 603
Horsham
West Sussex
RH13 5WL
UK

Helpline: 0844 324 6090
Website: www.rabbitwelfare.co.uk

House Rabbit Society
148 Broadway
Richmond
CA 94804

Website: www.rabbit.org.

Find the Author Online at:

www.rabbitrehome.org.uk

www.therabbithouse.com

Made in the USA
Middletown, DE
29 April 2020